GREEK MYTHOLOGY

ATHENA,

Goddess of Wisdom

BY JOANNA BLAIR

Enslow PUBLISHING

Please visit our website, www.enslow.com. For a free color catalog of all our high-quality books, call toll free 1-800-398-2504 or fax 1-877-980-4454.

Cataloging-in-Publication Data
Names: Blair, Joanna.
Title: Athena, goddess of wisdom / Joanna Blair.
Description: Buffalo, NY : Enslow Publishing, 2027. | Series: Greek mythology | Includes glossary and index.
Identifiers: ISBN 9781978550865 (pbk.) | ISBN 9781978550872 (library bound) | ISBN 9781978550889 (ebook)
Subjects: LCSH: Athena (Greek deity)--Juvenile literature. | Goddesses, Greek--Juvenile literature. | Mythology, Greek--Juvenile literature.
Classification: LCC BL820.M6 B535 2027 | DDC 292.2114--dc23

Published in 2027 by
Enslow Publishing
2544 Clinton Street
Buffalo, NY 14224

Portions of this work were originally authored by Christine Ha and published as *Athena*. All new material in this edition was authored by Joanna Blair.

Cover Designer: Joshua Olson
Interior Designer: Joshua Olson
Editor: Claire Vanden Branden

Photo Credits: Cover, p. 1 Daria Zelenska/Shutterstock.com; pp. 4–5 Stefano Carocci Ph/Shutterstock.com; pp. 6–7 Wikimedia Commons; pp. 8–9 Los Angeles County Museum of Art; pp. 10–11 Inga Fortuna/Shutterstock.com; pp. 12–13, 29 Dimitrios P./Shutterstock.com; p. 14 delcarmat/Shutterstock.com; p. 15 smoxx/Shutterstock.com; pp. 16–17 Cromagnon/Shutterstock.com; pp. 18–19 Davide Catoni/Shutterstock.com; pp. 20–21 QBR/Shutterstock.com; pp. 22–23 Alex Bellik/Shutterstock.com; p. 24 Forn Studio/Shutterstock.com; p. 25 Yaroslaff/Shutterstock.com; pp. 26–27 Tilia Lucida/Shutterstock.com.

Printed in China

CPSIA compliance information: Batch #QS27ENS: For further information contact Enslow Publishing, at 1-800-398-2504.

TABLE OF CONTENTS

4

CHAPTER 1

ABOUT ATHENA

Athena was the goddess of war and wisdom. She was the daughter of Zeus. Her birth was unusual. She sprang from his forehead. And she was fully grown and wearing armor.

Athena was Zeus's oldest child and favorite daughter.

Athena was known for her **justice** and intelligence. She protected cities and armies. In battles, she often chose a side and helped it win.

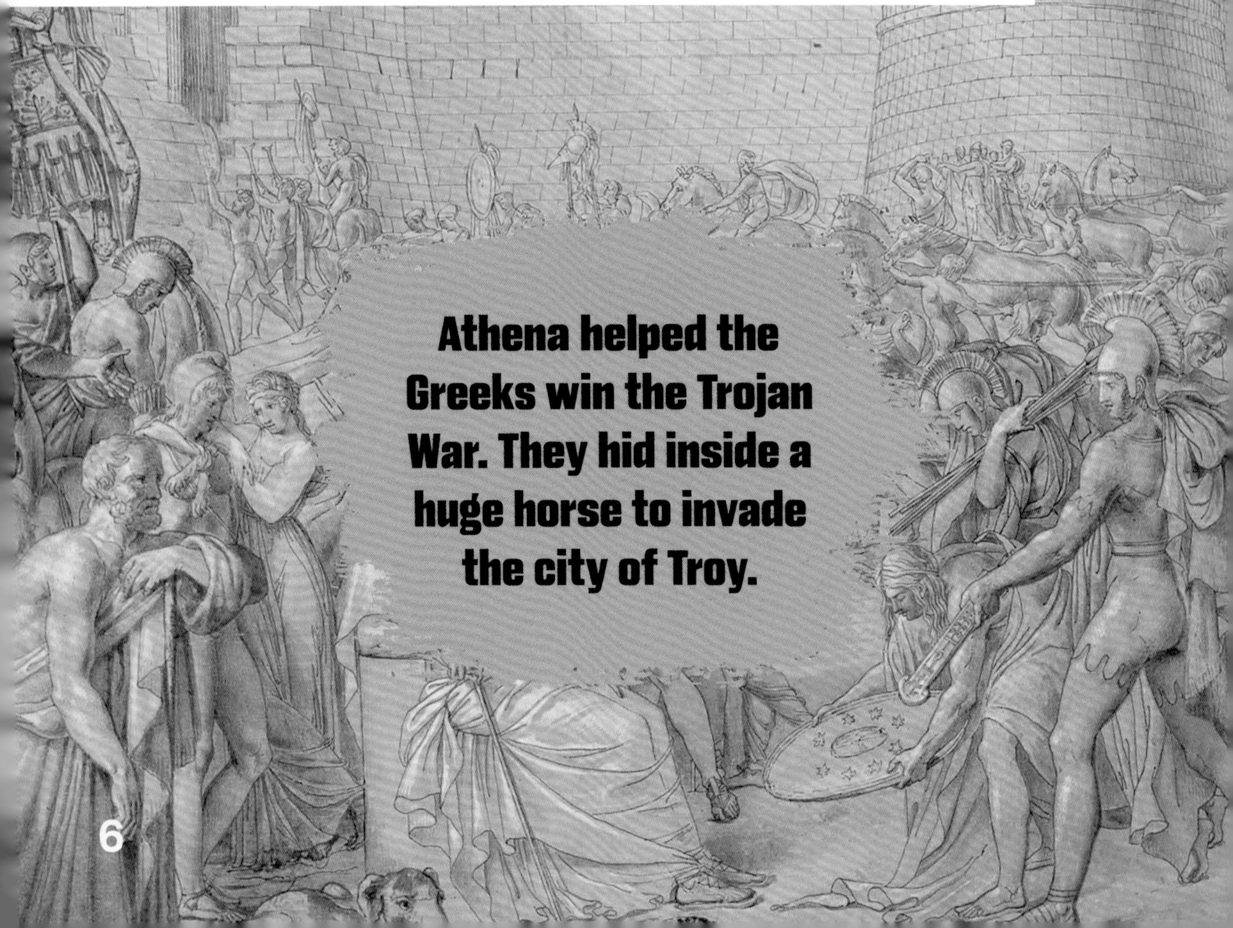

Athena helped the Greeks win the Trojan War. They hid inside a huge horse to invade the city of Troy.

Athena helped armies make plans to win battles.

ATHENA'S ANGER

When Athena got angry, she sometimes took **revenge**. In one story, Arachne bragged that her **spinning** was better than Athena's. Athena turned her into a spider.

The name Arachne means "spider" in Greek.

Athena was also a goddess of crafts. She was skilled at spinning and **weaving**.

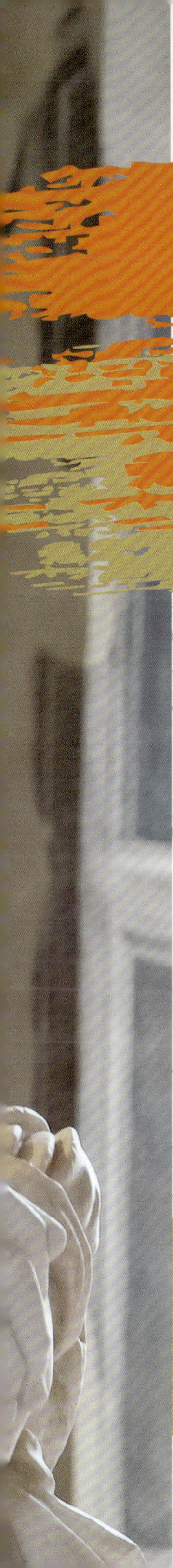

CHAPTER 2

FAMOUS MYTHS

Athena had a brother named Ares. He was the god of war. The two did not get along. Athena was calm and smart. Ares was angry and liked to fight.

Ares was disliked by many Greek gods.

Athena was born with her spear in her hand.

Sometimes Ares and Athena fought. She usually beat him. Athena defeated monsters, too. For example, she killed giants.

Athena often wore a helmet and armor. She carried a shield and a spear.

In several stories, Athena helped heroes. One was named Odysseus. He was shipwrecked. Athena sent someone to help him.

Athena helped the hero Jason capture a ram with golden fleece.

Odysseus sailed home to Ithaca. A statue of him stands on this island.

HEADING HOME

Athena helped Odysseus make a long journey home. She showed him what to do. And she guarded him from attacks.

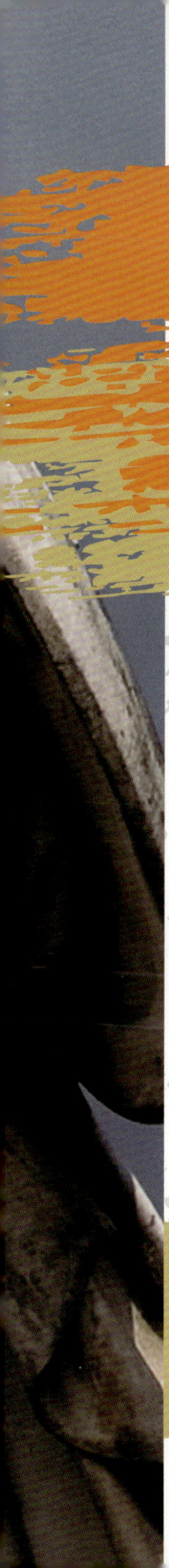

CHAPTER 3

A HELPFUL GODDESS

Athena could be **stern**. But she liked people who were brave. She helped and protected them.

Athena often gave heroes gifts or helped them fight.

For example, she helped Perseus defeat Medusa. Medusa could turn people to stone with one look.

Medusa was a monster with snakes for hair.

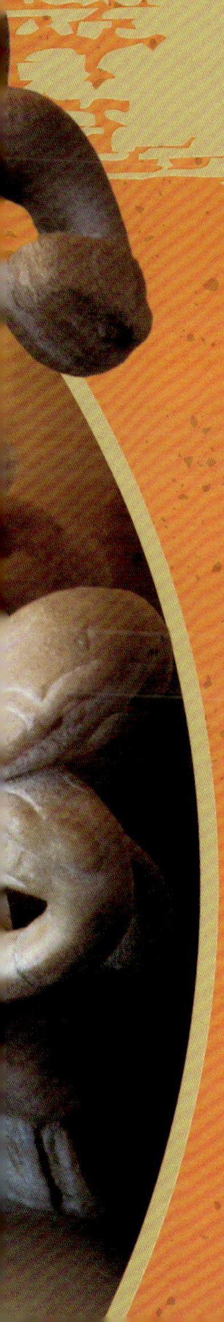

OTHER ADVENTURES

Athena gave Bellerophon a golden **bridle.** He used it to tame the winged horse Pegasus. Athena gave Hercules a golden sword. He used it to kill a monster.

The Greeks believed Athena invented many useful things. These items included ships, chariots, rakes, and plows.

In some myths, Athena's shield had Medusa's face on it. It could turn people to stone.

Athena gave Perseus a polished shield. He used it to watch Medusa's reflection. He sneaked up on the monster and killed her.

The hero Jason sailed on a ship called the *Argo*. Athena helped create it.

CHAPTER 4

HONORED BY ATHENS

Athena was the **guardian** of the city of Athens. She and Poseidon had both wanted this position. So, they had a contest. Each gave the city a gift.

Athena is sometimes shown holding an owl.

Poseidon made a **spring**. Athena planted an olive tree. The city's king picked Athena. He named the city after her.

Olive trees were valuable. They could provide food, oil, and wood.

Athens had pictures of Athena and her symbols on its coins.

ATHENA'S SYMBOLS

Owls and snakes were symbols of Athena. In Greece, owls represented wisdom. Snakes represented **cautiousness.** Olive leaves could be signs of Athena, too.

The Parthenon is a famous temple to Athena. It was built on a hill in Athens.

The people of Athens built temples in Athena's honor. They also had a big festival each year. It included a parade, music, and sports.

One temple had a huge statue of Athena inside. She stood 38 feet (11.5 m) tall.

TEST YOUR KNOWLEDGE

Take this quiz to test your knowledge.

1. Write a few sentences explaining the main ideas of Chapter 2.

2. If you had been the ruler of Athens, would you have chosen Athena or Poseidon? Why?

3. What was one of Athena's skills?

   A. music
   B. weaving
   C. sports

4. Why might Athena sometimes be stern?

   A. Her sense of justice would make her enforce the rules.
   B. Her sense of pride would make her say rude things.
   C. Her fear of losing would make her act unwisely.

5. What does **invade** mean in this book?

*Athena helped the Greeks win the Trojan War. They hid inside a huge horse to **invade** the city of Troy.*

A. attack and take over
B. run away from
C. give lots of money to

6. What does **defeated** mean in this book?

*Sometimes Ares and Athena fought. She usually beat him. Athena **defeated** monsters, too.*

A. won against
B. lost to
C. prayed to

Answers can be found on page 32.

GLOSSARY

bridle
A set of straps that allow a person to control a horse.

cautiousness
Being careful and looking out for danger.

chariots
Two-wheeled carts pulled by horses or other animals.

guardian
A person who protects something or someone.

justice
Doing what is right and fair.

revenge
Getting back at someone who has caused hurt or anger.

spinning
Twisting material together to make a long thread.

spring
A place where water bubbles up from underground.

stern
Serious and firm, especially in making people follow the rules.

weaving
Making fabric by lacing threads or strips of material together.

FOR MORE INFORMATION

BOOKS

MacCarald, Clara. *Greek Mythology Goddesses*. San Diego, CA: BrightPoint Press, 2022.

Sanderson, Whitney. *Athena*. Minneapolis, MN: Abdo Publishing, 2022.

WEBSITES

Britannica Kids: Athena

kids.britannica.com/kids/article/Athena/352800

Read more about Athena.

National Geographic: The Gods and Goddesses of Ancient Greece!

natgeokids.com/nz/discover/history/greece/greek-gods/

Learn more about Greek gods and goddesses.

INDEX

Answer Key:
1. Answers will vary; 2. Answers will vary; 3. B; 4. A; 5. A; 6. A